A TALE OF TWO CITIES

by
Charles Dickens

Student Packet

Written by
Mary L. Dennis
Kathleen Millin

Contains masters for:

1	Anticipation Guide
1	Vocabulary List
5	Vocabulary Activities
1	Study Guide (127 questions)
6	Literary Analysis Activities
2	Critical Thinking Activities
1	Concurrent Time Line Activity
1	Film Review Activity
3	Vocabulary Quizzes
3	Comprehension Quizzes
2	Unit Exams (Levels 1 and 2)

PLUS Detailed Answer Key

Note

The text used to prepare this guide was the Signet Classic published by New American Library/Penguin Books. The page references may differ in other editions.

Please note: Please assess the appropriateness of this book for the age level and maturity of your students prior to reading and discussing it with your class.

ISBN 1-56137-433-4

To order, contact your local school supply store, or—

Novel Units, Inc.
P.O. Box 791610
San Antonio, TX 78279

Web site: www.educyberstor.com

Anticipation Guide

Write "A" next to statements with which you agree. If you disagree, write "D." If you're not sure, write "NS." After you have read the novel, look at your answers again and see if you want to change any of them.

_____ 1. It is fitting and just that the middle and lower classes pay taxes so that those in power can live luxurious lifestyles.

_____ 2. Most people would enjoy seeing someone die in a violent way.

_____ 3. Redemption can be a result of a loving act.

_____ 4. Love and romance are the same thing.

_____ 5. Everyone is capable of murder under the right circumstances.

_____ 6. If you love another person enough, you can help them to heal physical, spiritual, and emotional wounds.

_____ 7. You are responsible for crimes committed by other members of your family.

_____ 8. Revolutions are usually successful because the new government treats people so much better than the previous government did.

_____ 9. Alcoholism is an insurmountable problem, and there is no way for an alcoholic to redeem him/herself.

_____10. Many people are capable of savage behavior.

Looking at just the front and back covers of *A Tale of Two Cities*, make a few notes in the space below on what you expect the book to be about. If you have seen the film version or read the book before, summarize below what you remember about it.

Vocabulary List
The words in the lists below are used in the Vocabulary Activities.

Book the First

epoch 13
requisition 15
perpetuation 21
restoratives 35
garret 44

incredulity 13
blunderbuss 17
ale-house 22
cadaverous 37
salutation 47

tumbril 14
adjuration 18
methodical 26
modicum 38
haggard 47

potentate 14
inexorable 21
sonorous 26
implacable 40
gaoler 51

Book the Second

Chapters 1-10
trepidation 64
bestrewn 71
acquitted 85
ignobly 110

reversionary 66
sublime 73
laconic 90
malady 122

quartering 67
pernicious 74
unscrupulous 92
renounce 129

illustrious 71
fervent 85
sultry 107

Chapters 11-24
gallantry 142
degradation 154
docile 180
turnkey 217

incorrigible 143
urchin 156
consecrated 188
impassive 219

magnanimous 144
dubious 166
sagacity 197
exultant 219

morose 152
repast 168
fidelity 205

Book the Third

Chapters 1-7
capricious 245
submissive 259
carnage 267
reiterated 281

functionary 246
armoury 261
fraternity 272
purveyors 285

emigrant 246
repudiated 262
avocations 272

commiseration 254
acquiescence 265
comely 273

Chapters 8-15
meddlesome 291
imperious 314
recognisant 329
ruthless 353

estranged 292
lamenting 324
inveteracy 337
insatiate 362

dissonance 298
anathematised 326
cautionary 342
rapacious 362

prevaricate 302
augment 327
juncture 350
prophetic 366

Directions: In the boxes, write the word from the list for <u>Book the First</u> that matches the definition. Then read vertically to find the names of three important characters, and write the names of the characters at the bottom of the page.

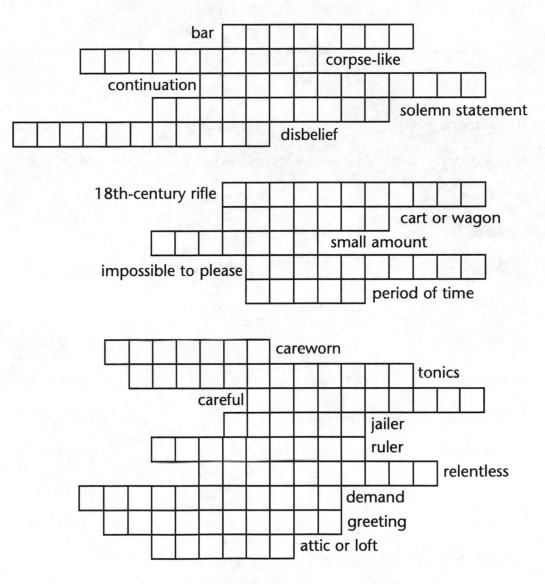

The characters hidden in the puzzle are:

_____, _____, and _____.

Directions: On each line below, circle the **one** word that does not belong with the others. The words that go together do not have to be synonyms, but they must be related in some way.

Example: illustrious - brilliant - artwork - genius

The word that does not belong is **artwork**. *Illustrious, brilliant,* and *genius* are all descriptive adjectives.

1. trepidation	fear	agitation	composure
2. reversionary	previous	revision	return
3. quartering	agony	currency	death
4. bestrewn	tidy	scattered	thrown
5. sublime	imprisoned	elevated	grand
6. pernicious	innocuous	rattlesnake	fatal
7. fervent	zealous	motivated	dispassionate
8. acquitted	defendant	plaintiff	exonerated
9. laconic	loquacious	terse	concise
10. unscrupulous	criminal	dishonest	precise
11. sultry	subarctic	jungle	stifling
12. ignobly	aristocracy	inferior	unworthy
13. malady	illness	invalid	barrister
14. renounce	microphone	relinquish	abandon

gallantry 142	incorrigible 143	magnanimous 144	morose 152
degradation 154	urchin 156	dubious 166	repast 168
docile 180	consecrated 188	sagacity 197	fidelity 205
turnkey 217	impassive 219	exultant 219	

Directions: Divide the words in the list above with two other students, so that each of you is responsible for five words. Make word maps for your words following the format below. (Use the back of your paper to draw the other maps.) When you have all finished your maps, share them with each other.

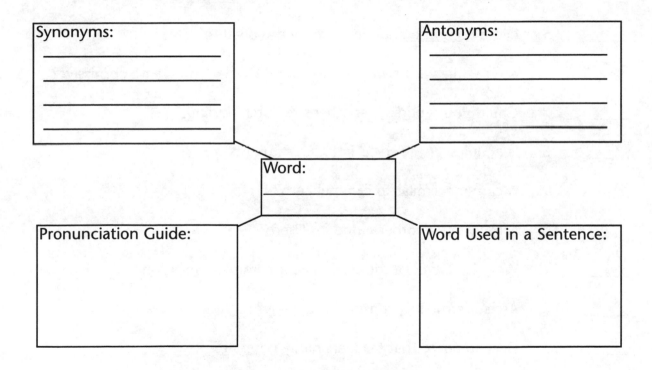

Synonyms:

Antonyms:

Word:

Pronunciation Guide:

Word Used in a Sentence:

Name_____

In the sentences below, the vocabulary words for Book the Third, Chapters 1-7 are underlined. Answer each of the questions below by writing "yes" or "no" on the line provided. If you answer "no," explain <u>why</u> in a brief statement under the sentence. The first one is done for you.

NO   1.   Is an <u>armoury</u> a piece of furniture used for storing clothing?

Weapons are stored in an armoury. Clothes are stored in an armoire.

_____   2.   Would it be <u>capricious</u> to sell your possessions and move to Tahiti?

_____   3.   Can a toll-booth attendant be considered a <u>functionary</u>?

_____   4.   Would you be able to view a display of <u>emigrants</u> at the zoo?

_____   5.   Did a <u>commiseration</u> investigate the death of JFK?

_____   6.   Are people who always go along with what you want <u>submissive</u>?

_____   7.   Could you <u>repudiate</u> another's research findings?

_____   8.   Is <u>acquiescence</u> served in fine restaurants?

_____   9.   Is <u>carnage</u> similar to caramel corn?

_____   10. Is <u>fraternity</u> another name for liberty?

_____   11. Would you take a trip during your summer <u>avocation</u>?

_____   12. Are supermodels considered <u>comely</u>?

_____   13. Do you agree that teachers rarely <u>reiterate</u>?

_____   14. Is the owner of a corner fruit stand a <u>purveyor</u>?

Directions: Next to each vocabulary word, write a synonym from the synonym box below.

Synonyms			
unappeasable	joining	grasping	lie
overbearing	separated	heartless	sorrowful
interfering	disagreement	cursed	intensify
aware	firmness	warning	predictive

1. meddlesome   _____

2. estranged   _____

3. dissonance   _____

4. prevaricate   _____

5. imperious   _____

6. lamenting   _____

7. anathematised   _____

8. augment   _____

9. recognisant   _____

10. inveteracy   _____

11. cautionary   _____

12. juncture   _____

13. ruthless   _____

14. insatiate   _____

15. rapacious   _____

16. prophetic   _____

Name_____

A Tale of Two Cities
Study Guide

Answer each question briefly but completely.

Book the First

Chapter One
1. Who are "the Woodman" and "the Farmer"?
2. What do you think the "certain movable framework" is?

Chapter Two
3. What is the mood of this chapter?
4. What do you think the phrase "recalled to life" means?

Chapter Three
5. Does the author feel humans trust one another?
6. Describe Jerry Cruncher.
7. What could "buried alive for 18 years" mean besides the literal and impossible?

Chapter Four
8. Explain what happened to Lucie when she was a small child.
9. Who is Miss Pross?

Chapter Five
10. What symbolic meaning is there in the spilled wine?
11. What is the Jacquerie?
12. In what activity is Mme. Defarge constantly engaged?

Chapter Six
13. What is Lucie's reaction to her father?
14. Does Dr. Manette want to be recalled to life?

Book the Second

Chapter One
1. Describe Tellson's Bank.
2. What job did Jerry perform for the bank?
3. What did Jerry object to his wife doing?

© Novel Units, Inc.

10

Chapter Two
4. What is the Old Bailey?
5. Describe Charles Darnay. Of what is he accused?
6. What were the people in the courtroom hoping for?

Chapter Three
7. Who are John Barsad and Roger Cly? Would you want them for friends?
8. Explain how Stryver was able to get Darnay acquitted.

Chapter Four
9. What is still bothering Dr. Manette?
10. Why did Mr. Lorry become angry with Mr. Carton?

Chapter Five
11. What is the relationship of Stryver and Carton?
12. Why is Carton so disconsolate?
13. How do you feel about Carton?

Chapter Six
14. Who lives in a house by Soho Square?
15. How does Dr. Manette now spend his days?
16. Who is Solomon, and what happened to him?
17. What upsetting news did Charles bring Dr. Manette?

Chapter Seven
18. What does the chocolate in this chapter symbolize?
19. What tragic accident took place in Saint Antoine?
20. What did the Defarges do in this chapter?

Chapter Eight
21. Explain (p. 119) "...until the wonder was that there was any village left unswallowed."
22. What adjectives and phrases describe the life of a peasant?

Chapter Nine
23. Who is the nephew of the Marquis?
24. How are the Marquis and his nephew different?
25. What happens to the Marquis at the end of this chapter?

Chapter 10
26. How much time has now passed since Lorry received the message about Dr. Manette?

27. How is Charles Darnay making a living? Why must he work?
28. What promise does Darnay make to Dr. Manette?
29. What does Dr. Manette do after Charles leaves?

Chapter 11
30. What do we learn about Stryver in this chapter?
31. Does Stryver seem humorous to you, or just odd? Why?

Chapter 12
32. What news did Mr. Lorry have for Stryver?

Chapter 13
33. What does Carton ask of Lucie?
34. What does Carton's confession reveal about his personality?
35. What promise does Carton make to Lucie?

Chapter 14
36. Whose funeral occurs in this chapter?
37. What does Jerry Cruncher do for his second income?
38. Why do you think Jerry beat his wife in this chapter?

Chapter 15
39. What story does the mender of roads relate?
40. What kind of mood does Jacques Three create?
41. What is decided about the "château and all its race"?

Chapter 16
42. Who came into the wine shop?
43. Does Mme. Defarge trust him? How do you know?
44. What surprising news does he bring?
45. Is Charles in danger? Why?

Chapter 17
46. How does Lucie's father feel about her marriage?
47. Where will Dr. Manette live after the wedding?

Chapter 18
48. What did Charles tell Dr. Manette the morning of the wedding? How did it affect the doctor? Why do you think he reacted this way?

49. Why do you think Mr. Lorry decided not to inform Lucie about her father's condition?

Chapter 19
50. Describe the approach Mr. Lorry used to tell Dr. Manette what had happened to him.
51. Do you think it was a good idea for Dr. Manette to give up his shoemaking tools?

Chapter 20
52. What did Sydney Carton ask of Darnay? Why do you think this was important to him?
53. What did Lucie have to say about Carton? What did she ask of Charles?

Chapter 21
54. How many children have Lucie and Charles had? What tragedy occurred involving one of the children?
55. What happens in France during this chapter?
56. Why do you think Defarge searched 105 North Tower?
57. Describe Mme. Defarge's actions in this chapter.

Chapter 22
58. Who is The Vengeance?
59. Why was Foulon hated so much?

Chapter 23
60. Are the problems in France over? What conditions exist?
61. Why didn't any of the villagers try to control the fire at the château?
62. Who is Gabelle? What happened to him?

Chapter 24
63. How many years have passed since the storming of the Bastille?
64. What had many of the displaced gentry in France done?
65. What has Mr. Lorry decided to do?
66. Who writes to Charles from France? What does he want?
67. What is Charles' "Loadstone Rock"?

Book the Third

Chapter One
1. Why is Darnay arrested? Where is he taken? By whose orders?
2. What insight does Charles' imprisonment give him?

Chapter Two
3. What surprises Mr. Lorry in this chapter?
4. What does Dr. Manette try to do?
5. What gruesome scene does Mr. Lorry keep Lucie from seeing?

Chapter Three
6. Why did Mr. Lorry find different lodgings for the Manettes?
7. Who brought the message from Dr. Manette to Lorry? What was it?
8. How did Lucie react to Mme. Defarge?
9. Why is Mme. Defarge so unsympathetic?

Chapter Four
10. What information was concealed from Lucie?
11. How has Dr. Manette changed?
12. How much time has elapsed since Charles was sent to prison?
13. What are the conditions in France now?

Chapter Five
14. What fear does Lucie have on page 272? Do you think she's right?
15. Where does Lucie go every day?
16. What is the Carmagnole? Why does it scare Lucie so much?

Chapter Six
17. For what reasons is Charles released?
18. What was the crowd's response to the acquittal?

Chapter Seven
19. Why didn't the family leave Paris as soon as Charles was released?
20. Why is Charles re-arrested?

Chapter Eight
21. Who do Miss Pross and Jerry meet while they are shopping?
22. What does Carton reveal about Solomon Pross?
23. What was buried in Cly's coffin?
24. Where does Solomon work?

Chapter Nine
25. What deal does Carton make with Solomon/Barsad?
26. Does Carton reveal his plans to anyone?
27. Why do you think he bought the drugs from the chemist?
28. What three people have denounced Charles?

Chapter 10
29. Summarize Dr. Manette's letter.
30. Do you think the situation is now hopeless? Will Charles die?

Chapter 11
31. Does Charles blame Dr. Manette for the letter?
32. What does Sydney Carton whisper to Lucie? What do you think he means?

Chapter 12
33. What does Mme. Defarge find curious about Carton?
34. What special reason does she have for wanting Charles to die?
35. Who else is in danger?
36. How has Dr. Manette handled the announcement of Charles' impending death?
37. What instructions does Carton give Mr. Lorry?

Chapter 13
38. Do you find it strange that Charles never thought of Carton when he was writing his letters?
39. Explain Carton's plan for Charles to escape.
40. What is the significance of the seamstress who is also going to the Guillotine?

Chapter 14
41. What humor does Dickens add at this very tense point in the novel?
42. Why did Mme. Defarge come to Lucie's house?
43. What did Miss Pross do? Was she justified?

Chapter 15
44. Does anyone, besides Miss Pross, know that Mme. Defarge is dead?
45. Explain: "Crush humanity out of shape once more, under similar hammers, and it will twist itself into the same tortured forms."
46. Do you think Carton died with a peaceful heart? Why?

**Think about the theme(s) in the novel. Make some notes
on what you feel Dickens was trying to say. Be prepared
to discuss your thoughts and feelings in class.**

Name_____

Directions: From the list below choose a word that fits into one of the categories: a definition, a word that completes a sentence, or an antonym.

epoch	*incredulity*	*tumbril*	*potentate*
requisition	*blunderbuss*	*adjuration*	*inexorable*
perpetuation	*ale-house*	*methodical*	*sonorous*
restoratives	*cadaverous*	*modicum*	*implacable*
garret	*salutation*	*haggard*	*gaoler*

Definitions:

1. tonics   _____
2. disbelief   _____
3. period of time   _____
4. solemn statement   _____
5. pale; weak   _____
6. bar   _____
7. jailer   _____

Sentences:

8. He raised his _____ and growled, "Don't move or I'll shoot!"
9. The _____ was full of newly-harvested corn.
10. The _____whisper of the wind in the trees was soothing.
11. The lieutenant sent in a _____ for more medical supplies.
12. He worked more slowly than other students, but was very _____.
13. The two words on the list which mean almost the same thing are _____
14. and _____.

Antonyms:

15. basement   _____
16. vibrant   _____
17. large amount   _____
18. discontinuation   _____
19. peasant   _____
20. farewell   _____

I. **Directions:** Write "Y" if the underlined word is used correctly. Write "N" if it is used incorrectly.

_____ 1. With considerable <u>trepidation</u>, Tim prepared to climb Denali.

_____ 2. Jeremy <u>acquitted</u> his summer job at McDonald's when school started.

_____ 3. Due to his <u>sublime</u> activities, he was court-martialed and jailed.

_____ 4. Many students missed school due to some <u>malady</u>.

_____ 5. We can thank Thomas Edison for our <u>illustrious</u> homes.

_____ 6. Although he was <u>unscrupulous</u>, the mayor was elected again and again.

_____ 7. The path through the forest was <u>bestrewn</u> with pinecones.

_____ 8. She was so <u>laconic</u> that few people were able to talk to her.

_____ 9. George fought his way through the <u>sultry</u> blizzard.

_____ 10. The sun shone brightly on another <u>pernicious</u> day that promised all sorts of good things.

II. **Match the words on the right with their correct definitions on the left.**

_____ 11. dedicated to a purpose   a. gallantry

_____ 12. wisdom   b. degradation

_____ 13. sad   c. consecrated

_____ 14. beyond reform   d. impassive

_____ 15. bravery   e. sagacity

_____ 16. loyalty; strength   f. fidelity

_____ 17. meal   g. morose

_____ 18. debasement   h. repast

_____ 19. overjoyed   i. incorrigible

_____ 20. calm   j. exultant

I. Choose the BEST definition for each word.

1. SUBMISSIVE a. sunken   b. obedient   c. rigid

2. REITERATED a. resented b. resembled c. repeated

3. FRATERNITY a. brotherhood b. frenzy   c. evocation

4. AVOCATIONS a. holidays b. hobbies   c. speeches

5. COMMISERATION a. pity   b. society   c. social system

6. ACQUIESCENCE a. wisdom b. agreement c. watery

7. MEDDLESOME a. awesome b. quarrelsome c. interfering

8. RUTHLESS   a. merciless b. rusty   c. poor

9. IMPERIOUS   a. royal   b. domineering c. impassive

10. INSATIATE   a. greedy   b. careful   c. prone

III. Choose FIVE of the words listed below. Write a sentence for each one.

capricious	functionary	emigrant	armoury
repudiated	carnage	comely	purveyors
recognisant	estranged	lamenting	inveteracy
dissonance	anathematised	cautionary	rapacious
prevaricate	augment	juncture	prophetic

11. _____

  _____

12. _____

  _____

13. _____

  _____

14. _____

  _____

15. _____

  _____

Name_____

Directions: As you read *A Tale of Two Cities,* fill in the Character Charts below and on the next page. This will greatly aid your understanding of the novel.

Character	Physical Description	Wants Most:	Good or Evil?	Memorable Quote
Jarvis Lorry				
Jerry Cruncher				
Lucie Manette				
Doctor Manette				
Monsieur Defarge				

Name_____

Character	Physical Description	Wants Most:	Good or Evil?	Memorable Quote
Madame Defarge				
Sydney Carton				
Charles Darnay				
John Barsad				
Miss Pross				

Directions: If you have ever watched a television program that was presented in several parts, you probably groaned when the screen read "To Be Continued." In the same way, Dickens tried to leave his readers "on the edge of their chairs" waiting for the next installment of his novel to appear. As you read the novel, record below the moments of dramatic suspense where you would choose to divide the novel into parts. You should identify at least five of these suspenseful moments. If you'd like, use another sheet of paper to break the novel down even further. (Dickens' readers would have been given only one or two chapters in each installment.)

Divide After: (Book #, Chapter)	What action has just occurred? What questions are left in the mind of the reader?

Authors often use a technique called **foreshadowing** to create suspense by giving the reader a hint of something that will happen later on in the story. As you read the novel, note instances of foreshadowing on the chart below. When you have finished the novel, you can review your chart and see how observant you were of the author's hints.

Page #	Foreshadowing Statement or Event	What I Think Will Happen

Name_____

Directions: On the right is a listing of some actual historical events from the time the novel begins, 1775, to the year the novel ends, 1793. On the left, fill in the main events from the novel for the corresponding time frames. (You will not have novel events for all the years.)

Actual Historical Events		A Tale of Two Cities Events
The Revolutionary War breaks out in America, and British troops are sent to quell the rebellion—which they find they are unable to do.	**1775**	
The Declaration of Independence is signed.	**1776**	
France makes an alliance with the new United States of America.	**1778**	
The war causes a sharp increase in France's deficit.	**1780**	
France's finance minister is dismissed from office, revealing the desperate state of French finances. Heavy taxes are levied on the poor.	**1781**	
France moves toward revolution because of its financial crisis.	**1787**	
The French Revolution begins when Parisian mob storms the Bastille.	**1789**	
The French royal family is imprisoned; the New Republic of France is at war with Austria and Prussia.	**1792**	
King Louis XVI and Marie Antoinette are executed. Robespierre rises to power in France. The Reign of Terror begins.	**1793**	

Directions: Just as we make decisions that affect our lives, characters in novels make decisions that result in complications and conflicts which carry the story forward. At the end of <u>Book the Second</u>, Charles Darnay decides he must go to France to help Gabelle…but what if Charles had decided to ignore Gabelle's pleas, and had stayed home in England with his family? Next to each character below, indicate how this alternate decision would probably have affected the character. The first one is done as an example.

1. Dr. Manette: *would never have been able to come to terms with his former imprisonment; might not have realized that things had gotten out of hand in France and probably would have remained in sympathy with the revolutionaries.*

2. Miss Pross:

3. Lucie:

4. Sydney Carton:

5. Jarvis Lorry:

6. Jerry Cruncher:

7. Madame Defarge:

Directions: Many kinds of love are represented in *A Tale of Two Cities*. With your group, discuss the various examples and note them on the chart below. Share your group's conclusions with the rest of the class.

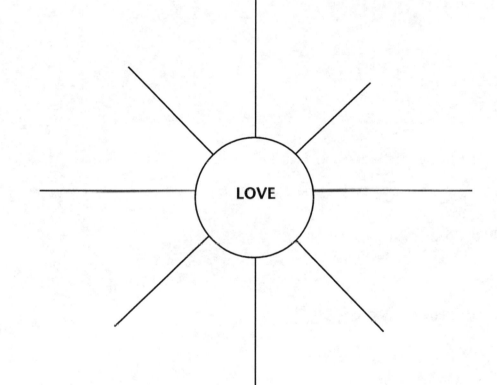

Directions: Dickens often uses **figurative language** in his writing—not just simple similes and metaphors, but extended metaphors, personification, and elaborate imagery pages. The main subjects for some examples of figurative language from *A Tale of Two Cities* are listed below. For each one, indicate the comparisons the figurative section makes.

1. page 38: the mill

2. page 38: Hunger

3. page 62: Death

4. Book Two, Chapter 5: the lion and the jackal

5. Book Two, Chapter 7: Monseigneur

6. Book Two, Chapter 21: echoes

7. Book Three, Chapter 2: the grindstone

8. Book Three, Chapter 8: the card game

Stories are built on cause-and-effect relationships. An event (cause) leads to a result (effect), which then becomes a cause of another effect. If you get nervous about taking tests, you can see how cause-and-effect works:

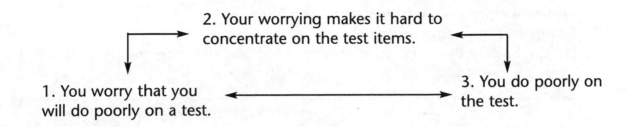

2. Your worrying makes it hard to concentrate on the test items.

1. You worry that you will do poorly on a test.

3. You do poorly on the test.

In *A Tale of Two Cities,* the root <u>cause</u> of the final result goes back to the actions of the Evrémonde family toward a poor peasant family. Beginning there, trace the causes and effects that lead to the results.

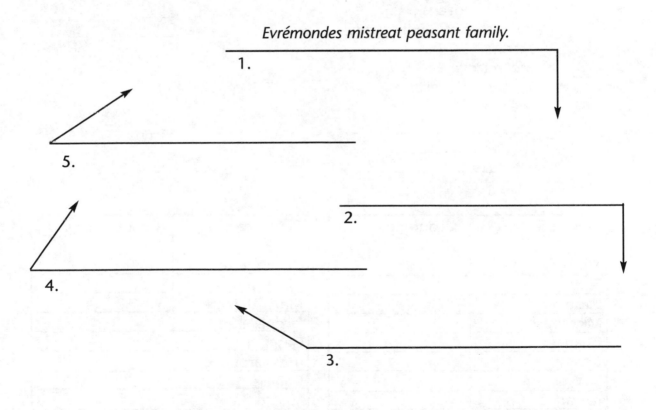

Evrémondes mistreat peasant family.

1.

5.

2.

4.

3.

Name_____

Directions: Similarities among characters are sometimes a clue to themes in the story.
1. Think about how many ways you can group the characters in the novel based on some common element.
2. Add your own groupings to those listed below.
3. Assign each grouping a symbol (the first three are done).
4. List symbols by each character's name to indicate all of the groupings to which he or she belongs.

Names of Groupings	Symbols for Groupings
women	#
men	*
French citizens	+
English citizens	____
members of the Jacquerie	____
victims	____
victimizers	____
adds comic relief	____
wealthy	____
_____	____
_____	____
_____	____

Character	Groupings	Character	Groupings
Mr. Lorry		Dr. Manette	
Jerry		M. Defarge	
Lucie		Mme. Defarge	
Miss Pross		Jacques 3	
Charles		Gaspard	
Carton		the Marquis	
Stryver		Gabelle	
Barsad		Foulon	
Gaspard		Gaspard	

Name_____

You're the Critic

Before Viewing

1. Imagine you are a screenwriter (the person who writes the script for the movie) for *A Tale of Two Cities*. List below the five scenes which will be the most important in your movie.

   a.

   b.

   c.

   d.

   e.

After Viewing

2. Did the screenwriter include the scenes you listed above? Which scene in the movie do you think is the most memorable?

3. Did you view the movie in color or black and white? Do you think it could be more effective if done the other way?

4. Did the actors and actresses portray the characters as you imagined them when you were reading the book? If so, what was especially good about them? If not, to what did you object?

5. If you were choosing a cast of characters from your favorites, who would play the leading roles? Give reasons for your choices.

6. Overall, how could the film be improved?

I. **Character Match:** Characters may be used more than once.

_____ 1. brings message from Tellson's
_____ 2. wife of the wine-shop owner
_____ 3. compassionate 17-year-old
_____ 4. King of France
_____ 5. takes daughter to her father
_____ 6. once imprisoned in Bastille
_____ 7. tells a daughter her father is alive
_____ 8. former servant to a doctor
_____ 9. King of England
_____ 10. constantly knitting

A. Jarvis Lorry
B. Jerry Cruncher
C. Lucie Manette
D. Dr. Manette
E. Monsieur Defarge
F. Madame Defarge
G. Louis XVI
H. George III

II. **Multiple Choice:** Choose the BEST answer.

11. The MAIN problem afflicting the citizens of St. Antoine is
   A. disease   B. poor housing   C. ignorance   D. hunger

12. Lorry's reply to the message he received on the Dover Road is
   A. "See you in Paris."   C. "Recalled to life."
   B. "I've been robbed."   D. "Wait at Dover for Mam'selle."

13. When the doctor first sees his daughter, he immediately
   A. wants to leave for London   C. shows her a pair of shoes he made
   B. recognizes her   D. asks if she's the gaoler's daughter

14. The spilled wine in the streets of Saint Antoine symbolizes
   A. the coming Revolution   C. the desperation of the people
   B. spilled blood   D. all of these

15. The secret name used by members of the revolutionary society is
   A. Jean-Claude   B. Pierre   C. Paul   D. Jacques

I. Matching. Some letters may be used more than once.

_____1. "the triumphant perfection of inconvenience"
_____2. hopelessly professes his love to Lucie
_____3. His carriage kills a child.
_____4. has a coded register of names
_____5. a "patriot" who testifies against Darnay
_____6. decides not to marry Lucie
_____7. location of the Manette home
_____8. searches 105 North Tower
_____9. sends a message for help to Charles
_____10. courtroom
_____11. nephew of the Marquis
_____12. reverts to shoe-making when stressed
_____13. often has premonitions about the future
_____14. acquitted of treason
_____15. Her son died.

A. the Marquis
B. Old Bailey
C. Mr. Stryver
D. Dr. Manette
E. Charles Darnay
F. Madame Defarge
G. Tellson's Bank
H. Soho
I. Lucie
J. Monsieur Defarge
K. John Barsad
L. Gabelle
M. Sydney Carton

II. True-False.

_____ 16. Jerry's muddy boots are a clue to his night-time profession.

_____ 17. The Marquis gave Gaspard a gold watch to placate him.

_____ 18. Dr. Manette was thrilled to find out Charles wanted to marry Lucie.

_____ 19. Lucie asked Charles not to speak ill of Carton.

_____ 20. The Marquis was murdered by Charles, who wanted the château.

_____ 21. Jerry Cruncher's son learned of his father's job as a "resurrection man."

_____ 22. Charles Darnay and Sydney Carton resemble one another in appearance.

_____ 23. The château was burned per Charles' orders.

_____ 24. After the Revolution, there was plenty of food for everyone.

_____ 25. The author of this novel is Carl Dickens.

Name_____

I. **Matching.** Match each quote with its speaker.

_____ 1. "Down with the emigrant!"

_____ 2. "Thank God that no one near and dear to me is in this town tonight!"

_____ 3. "Oh Solomon, dear Solomon!"

_____ 4. "Don't go and tell *me* that you buried Cly."

_____ 5. "You will be careful to keep them separate, citizen? You know the consequences of mixing them?"

_____ 6. "He made shoes, he made shoes, he made shoes."

_____ 7. "What? Walking here again, citizeness?"

_____ 8. "A life you love!"

_____ 9. "Your suspense is nearly ended, my darling; he shall be restored to you within a few hours."

_____ 10. "O sister-woman, think of me. As a wife and mother."

A. Lucie
B. the wood sawyer
C. Charles Darnay
D. the chemist
E. Dr. Manette
F. Jarvis Lorry
G. Miss Pross
H. peasants in Beauvais
I. Jerry Cruncher
J. Sydney Carton

II. **Sequencing.** Number each set of events in chronological order.

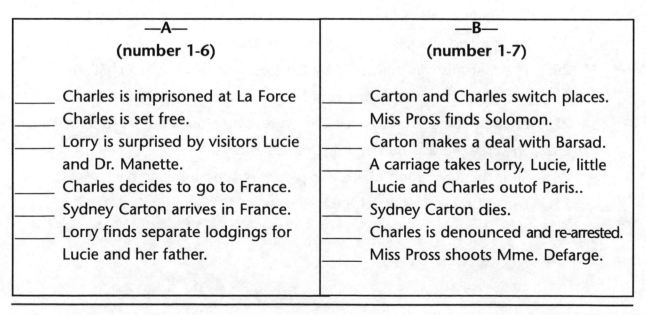

—A— (number 1-6)	—B— (number 1-7)
_____ Charles is imprisoned at La Force	_____ Carton and Charles switch places.
_____ Charles is set free.	_____ Miss Pross finds Solomon.
_____ Lorry is surprised by visitors Lucie and Dr. Manette.	_____ Carton makes a deal with Barsad.
_____ Charles decides to go to France.	_____ A carriage takes Lorry, Lucie, little Lucie and Charles out of Paris..
_____ Sydney Carton arrives in France.	_____ Sydney Carton dies.
_____ Lorry finds separate lodgings for Lucie and her father.	_____ Charles is denounced and re-arrested.
	_____ Miss Pross shoots Mme. Defarge.

True-False.

_____ 1. The "two cities" in the title are Dover and Saint Antoine.
_____ 2. This novel consists of three books.
_____ 3. All of the characters in the book are introduced in the first book.
_____ 4. The mood of this novel is often foreboding.
_____ 5. The Manette home is in Saint Antoine.
_____ 6. *A Tale of Two Cities* takes place over four years.
_____ 7. Many actual historical events are represented in this novel.
_____ 8. Chapter headings often foreshadow important events.
_____ 9. The story begins on the Dover Road.
_____ 10. *A Tale of Two Cities* was originally released in seven parts.

Multiple Choice.

11. The story opens in the year
    A. 1812   B. 1775   C. 1787   D. none of the above

12. Jerry Cruncher is given a reply to deliver. It reads
    A. "It is time."   B. "Acquitted."   C. "Recalled to life."   D. "Fear not."

13. The code name used by the French revolutionaries is
    A. Jacques   B. Ernest   C. Charles   D. Sydney

14. Jerry Cruncher's wife aggravates him by
    A. praying   B. shopping   C. knitting   D. arguing

15. In England, Darnay was charged with
    A. theft   B. forgery   C. treason   D. murder

16. Monsieur the Marquis rode in a carriage that killed
    A. an old man   B. Gabelle's son   C. a road mender   D. a child

17. Darnay is the Marquis'
    A. son   B. cousin   C. brother   D. nephew

18. Charles Darnay becomes a
    A. lawyer   B. teacher   C. wine-keeper   D. gaoler

19. Lucie is loved by
    A. Mme. Defarge   B. Solomon Pross   C. Sydney Carton   D. the Marquis

20. Madame Defarge's signal that a spy was in the room was
    A. putting her knitting away   C. putting a rose in her hair
    B. having a coughing fit   D. asking someone for the time

Matching.
Each chapter title on the left corresponds to an item in the right-hand column.

_____ 21. The Grindstone
_____ 22. The Honest Tradesman
_____ 23. The Gorgon's Head
_____ 24. The Jackal
_____ 25. The Knitting Done
_____ 26. Fifty-Two
_____ 27. Echoing Footsteps
_____ 28. The Fellow of Delicacy
_____ 29. A Hand at Cards
_____ 30. Drawn to the Loadstone Rock

A. Mme. Defarge dies
B. Charles leaves for France
C. Carton enlists Barsad's help
D. the Manette home
E. Jerry Cruncher
F. Mr. Lorry
G. Sydney Carton
H. revolutionaries prepare to murder the prisoners
I. beheadings
J. the Marquis dies

Fill in the Blank.

31. The Marquis threw a _____ at Gaspard.

32. Mr. Lorry's employer was _____.

33. Jerry Cruncher made extra money by _____ at night.

34. John Barsad's real name was _____.

35. The Vengeance _____ to gather the women.

36. Madame Defarge's register is in her _____.

37. Miss Pross kills Mme. Defarge with a _____.

38. Sydney Carton was killed by a _____.

39. Dr. Manette _____ while he was in prison and
even afterwards, when he was upset.

40. The purpose of Charles Darnay's trip to Paris was to help _____.

Short Essay.

41.-45. Explain why Madame Defarge despised the Evrémonde family so much. Be
specific.

46.-50. What part did Sydney Carton play in helping Lucie keep "a life she loved
beside her"?

USE SEPARATE PAPER TO WRITE YOUR ANSWERS FOR THIS TEST.

I. Brief Essay. Support each of the statements below with examples from the novel. If you don't agree with the statement, explain why.

1. Lucie Manette was a devoted daughter, friend, mother, and wife.
2. Dr. Manette suffered from his solitary confinement long after he was released.
3. What he left behind was more important to Sydney Carton than his own life.
4. Mr. Lorry was loyal to Tellson's Bank, but he was also sensitive and kind.

II. Critical Thinking/Writing. Consider the importance of each of the settings below. Write the topic sentence you would use if you were writing a paragraph about the function of each.

1. Tellson's Bank
2. The Old Bailey
3. The wine-shop
4. The château
5. 105 North Tower

Choose two of your topic sentences and complete the paragraphs.

III. Long Essay. Choose one topic below and write a well-organized essay.

1. One theme of *A Tale of Two Cities* is love's power of resurrection. Consider the characters Sydney Carton and Lucie Manette. How does each contribute to this theme?

2. Both Madame and Monsieur Defarge are devoted to the ideals of the French Revolution, yet their motives and actions differ. Explain how and why.

3. Jerry Cruncher, Miss Pross, John Barsad, and Doctor Manette seem like fairly minor characters, yet each plays an essential part in the novel. Explain the function of each.

Answer Key

Note: Some sample answers are given when there is no single "correct" answer. In the case of these open-ended questions, students should be given credit for any answers that can be justified.

Activities

Activity #1: Answers will vary, and should be shared with other students.

Activity #2: *Reading from the top:* alehouse, cadaverous, perpetuation, adjuration, incredulity, blunderbuss, tumbril, modicum, implacable, epoch, haggard, restoratives, methodical, gaoler, potentate, inexorable, requisition, salutation, garret. *Characters:* Lorry, Lucie, Dr. Manette (any order)

Activity #3: 1-composure, 2-revision, 3-currency, 4-tidy, 5-imprisoned, 6-innocuous, 7-dispassionate, 8-plaintiff, 9-loquacious, 10-precise, 11-subarctic, 12-aristocracy, 13-malady, 14-microphone.

Activity #4: Word maps will vary.

Activity #5: 1-no, 2-yes, 3-yes, 4-no; Emigrants are people who go to another country to live. 5-no; A commission did. 6-yes, 7-yes, 8-no; Acquiescence is agreement. 9-no; Carnage is the result of massacre. 10-no; It is another name for brotherhood. 11-no; An avocation is a hobby. 12-yes, 13-no; Teachers must often repeat themselves. 14-yes.

Activity #6: 1-interfering; 2-separated; 3-disagreement; 4-lie; 5-overbearing; 6-sorrowful; 7-cursed; 8-intensify, 9-aware; 10-firmness; 11-warning; 12-joining; 13-heartless; 14-unappeasable; 15-grasping; 16-predictive.

Activity #7: (sample answers; students' may vary) **Lorry** is a neat little man in a blonde wig who wants to tend to business and not offend or hurt anyone. He is a decidedly good character who might best be remembered for his reminder to himself "Business! Business!" **Jerry** is rather sinister-looking, with spiky hair around a bald spot. He is motivated by money, but also seems concerned about his son's future. He is more comic than evil, and might be remembered for telling Mr. Lorry he has been working as an "agricultooral character." **Lucie** is petite, blue-eyed, golden-haired. She seems to want most the happiness of those around her. She is a good character, and this is obvious in her memorable quote about Carton, "Remember how strong we are in our happiness and how weak he is in his misery." **Doctor Manette** is a white-haired, bent old man who wants most to keep his daughter near him and for her to be happy. He is a good character, and might be remembered for his indignant reply to the Tribunal, "I indignantly protest to you that this is a forgery and a fraud!" **Monsieur Defarge** is a "bull-necked martial-looking man of thirty" who wants the revolution to succeed. His intentions are good, but some students may see his actions as evil. He might be remembered for his entreaty to his wife, "…but one must stop somewhere." **Madame Defarge**, dark and stout, is obsessed with revenge on the Evrémondes. Although she is an evil character, her actions may seem justifiable. A typical quote: "I will tear you to pieces, but I will have you from that door." **Sydney Carton** and **Charles Darnay** look alike: handsome young men with dark hair; strangely, both want Lucie to be happy and safe. They are both good characters. Memorable quotes: Carton— "...there is a man who would give his life to keep a life you love beside you." Charles—"Don't add your death to the bitterness of mine." **John Barsad**, a.k.a. Solomon Pross, is a black-haired, aquiline-nosed, 40-ish character who wants only to make money. Memorable quote: (to Carton) "You swear not to betray me?" **Miss Pross**, wild-looking and red-haired, is motivated by her desire for Lucie's happiness. She is a good character who tells Madame Defarge "I know that the longer I keep you here, the greater hope there is for my Ladybird."

Activity #8: Students' answers will vary. To help them decide where to divide the novel, suggest they read the last few lines of chapters.

Activity #9: Students' answers and predictions will vary. Samples: p. 21—"You'd be in a Blazing bad way if recalling to life was to come into fashion, Jerry!" p. 38—"The time was to come when that wine too would be spilled..." p. 209 "...there would arise the sound of footsteps at her own early grave;"

Activity #10: (Students' answers may vary somewhat.) **1775:** Jarvis Lorry receives a message that Dr. Manette is alive. He takes Lucie to Paris and they bring her father back to London. **1780:** Charles Darnay is acquitted of treason. He, Carton, and Stryver see Lucie at the trial and all fall in love with her. Gaspard's child is killed; he in turn murders the Marquis, who we learn is Charles' uncle. Charles renounces his inheritance. **1781:** Charles asks Lucie's father if he may marry her. Stryver is driven off by Lorry. Sydney Carton tells Lucie he would give his life for her. **1789:** The Defarges take part in the revolution. Defarge searches 105 N. Tower. Mme. Defarge beheads a guard. **1792:** Charles goes to France to help Gabelle and is arrested. Lucie, her father, and Miss Pross go to France to help him. Lorry and Jerry are already there. **1793:** Charles is freed, then rearrested. Carton arrives in Paris, threatens Barsad into helping him, and dies in Charles' place.

Activity #11: 2-Miss Pross would not have gone to France, would not have killed Mme. Defarge, and would not have gone suddenly deaf. 3- Lucie would have continued her easy life in London. 3-Sydney Carton would not have given his life to save Charles; he might have died a disreputable drunk instead of a hero. 5-Jarvis Lorry would not have seen Carton in a new light. 6-Jerry Cruncher would not have divulged the secrets of his night-time job; might not have reformed. 7-Mme. Defarge would not have been killed.

Activity #12: Some types of love: father-daughter; guardian-charge; husband-wife; hopeless admirer-love object; friend-friend; father-child; brother-family; hero-crowd. Students should give examples of these. They may mention additional types and examples.

Activity #13: See sections referenced for class discussion of answers.

Activity #14: Students' answers should show an understanding of how one event leads to another.

Activity #15: Students' symbols and groupings will vary but should be accurate.

Activity #16: Students' answers will vary.

Study Guide

Book the First

1. The Woodman is Fate, the Farmer is Death.
2. the guillotine
3. tense, foreboding
4. various answers
5. no
6. close-together black eyes; sinister expression; spiky black hair around bald crown
7. various answers
8. She was taken from France to England and not told her father was in prison.
9. Lucie's guardian
10. spilled blood; the coming revolution
11. secret revolutionary society
12. knitting
13. She feels great compassion and love for him.
14. He is not sure.

Book the Second

1. old-fashioned, dark, ugly; "the triumphant perfection of inconvenience"
2. odd jobs; messenger
3. praying
4. courthouse
5. 25, handsome, dark hair and eyes
6. an execution
7. paid witnesses; probably not
8. by discrediting the witnesses
9. the memories of the time he spent in prison
10. Carton indicated he had no use for businessmen.
11. Stryver is the pompous barrister. Carton, who does the work, is ignored.
12. He feels very unworthy and discouraged about himself.
13. various answers
14. the Manettes
15. seeing patients
16. Miss Pross's brother. He took all her money and disappeared.
17. A letter had been found in an old dungeon.
18. The life of leisure led by the wealthy.
19. A child was killed by a racing carriage owned by the Marquis.
20. M. Defarge tries to comfort Gaspard; Mme. Defarge knits and watches.
21. The taxes on the poor had taken everything they had.
22. miserable, desolate, hopeless, meager, etc.
23. Charles Darnay
24. The Marquis is heartless and cold; Charles hates how the peasants are treated.
25. He is killed.
26. six years

---

27. teaching; He relinquished his inheritance.
28. He will reveal his family name on the morning of the wedding.
29. begins hammering at his shoemaker's bench
30. He also wants to marry Lucie.
31. various answers
32. He told him it might not be a good idea to propose.
33. to keep his confession a secret
34. He is sensitive, romantic, and has low self-esteem.
35. He will lay down his life for her or one she loves.
36. Roger Cly's
37. grave robbing
38. Apparently, the grave robbing didn't go as planned.
39. the grisly execution of Gaspard
40. one of anticipation for the revolution
41. They will all be exterminated.
42. John Barsad
43. No; she reveals nothing of her sympathy for the revolution.
44. that Lucie and Charles will marry
45. Yes; he is part of the "château and all its race."
46. Happy for her but sorry for himself.
47. at the house in Soho with Charles and Lucie
48. his true family name; he became pale and later had a relapse
49. various answers
50. He told him about a friend who had a problem.
51. various answers
52. to be friends with him; possibly to be close to Lucie
53. that he had potential; not to malign him
54. two; their son died
55. the revolution begins
56. various answers
57. leads the women; beheads a guard
58. Mme. Defarge's right-hand woman
59. He had once told the people they should eat grass.
60. No; there is chaos and people are still starving.
61. They enjoyed watching it burn.
62. the postmaster and caretaker of the château; captured and jailed
63. three
64. emigrated to England
65. go to France to protect the bank's interests
66. Gabelle wants Charles to help him get out of prison.
67. France

Book the Third
1. He is an emigrant. La Force prison. Defarge's.
2. He understands why Dr. Manette made shoes.

---

3. Lucie and Dr. Manette arrive.
4. help Charles get out of prison
5. the peasants sharpening their weapons of murder
6. He wanted to protect the bank.
7. Defarge. Charles is safe and there is hope.
8. She begged her to have pity, but was rebuffed. Then she grew very afraid.
9. She has seen so many other mothers and children killed by the aristocracy.
10. that there had been a murderous raid on the prison
11. He has found strength and purpose in his mission to help Charles.
12. one year
13. The people have gone nearly insane. (Historically, it is the Reign of Terror.)
14. She fears the wood-sawyer is a spy for the Defarge's. Yes.
15. to a corner where Charles might see her from the prison
16. the dance of the revolution; the wood-sawyer is in it
17. because he relinquished his inheritance and was married to the daughter of a patriot
18. They cheered.
19. It was dangerous to leave right away; it would look suspicious.
20. He has been denounced by three people.
21. Solomon, Miss Pross's brother
22. He is using a false name (Barsad), was once employed by the English and now by France, which makes him appear to be a counter-spy.
23. paving stones
24. at La Force prison
25. Carton will be admitted once to Charles' cell.
26. no
27. various answers
28. both Defarges and Dr. Manette
29. He was called to tend a raving peasant girl and her dying brother. The brother revealed how his sister's husband had been worked to death by the Evrémondes, the sister raped, the father dead of shock. When Manette tried to report the mistreatment to the authorities he was thrown in prison on orders of the Marquis Evrémonde.
30. various answers
31. no
32. "A life you love!" (Refer to page 156.)
33. He looks very much like Charles.
34. She is the surviving sister of the peasant family.
35. Lucie, little Lucie, and even Dr. Manette
36. He is looking for his shoemaking tools again.
37. to leave the instant he jumps in the carriage
38. various answers
39. Carton and Charles will exchange clothes. Carton will drug Charles to make it appear he fainted. Charles (masquerading as Carton) will be carried out of the prison.
40. She sees Carton as a hero and knows nothing else about him.

41. Jerry Cruncher insists on Miss Pross hearing his two vows—to give up his grave-robbing and not to interfere with his wife's praying.
42. to kill her herself
43. shot Mme. Defarge; Most will say yes.
44. no
45. Dickens is saying that revolution is always the result of exploiting people.
46. various answers

Vocabulary Quizzes

Book the First	Book the Second	Book the Third
1. restoratives	1. Y	1. B
2. incredulity	2. N	2. C
3. epoch	3. N	3. A
4. adjuration	4. Y	4. B
5. haggard	5. N	5. A
(or cadaverous)	6. Y	6. B
6. ale-house	7. Y	7. C
7. gaoler	8. Y	8. A
8. blunderbuss	9. N	9. B
9. tumbril	10. N	10. A
10. sonorous	11. C	11. -15. Will vary.
11. requisition	12. E	Check sentences for
12. methodical	13. G	accuracy.
13. inexorable	14. I	
14. implacable	15. A	(Offer bonus points
15. garret	16. F	to students who
16. cadaverous	17. H	choose more than
(or haggard)	18. B	five words.)
17. modicum	19. J	
18. perpetuation	20. D	
19. potentate		
20. salutation		

COMPREHENSION QUIZZES

Book the First	Book the Second		Book the Third
1. B	1. G	16. T	1. H
2. F	2. M	17. F	2. F
3. C	3. A	18. F	3. G
4. G	4. F	19. T	4. I
5. E	5. K	20. F	5. D
6. D	6. C	21. T	6. C
7. A	7. H	22. T	7. B
8. E	8. J	23. F	8. J
9. H	9. L	24. F	9. E
10. F	10. B	25. F	10. A
11. D	11. E		
12. C	12. D		SEQUENCE A: 2,5,3,1,6,4
13. D	13. I		
14. D	14. E		SEQUENCE B: 4,2,3,5,7,1,6
15. D	15. I		

Unit Test • Level I

1. F	11. B	21. H	31. gold coin	41.-45. She was the only surviving member of the peasant family abused by the Evrémondes.
2. T	12. C	22. E	32. Tellson's Bank	
3. F	13. A	23. J	33. grave-robbing	
4. T	14. A	24. G	34. Solomon Pross	
5. F	15. C	25. A	35. beats a drum	
6. F	16. D	26. I	36. knitting	46.-50. He switched places with Charles and died instead of him.
7. T	17. D	27. D	37. gun	
8. T	18. B	28. F	38. guillotine	
9. T	19. C	29. C	39. made shoes	
10. F	20. C	30. B	40. Gabelle	

UNIT TEST • LEVEL II

Answers to this test are fairly open to interpretation by the students and should be graded according to your own standards.